MIKE JOHNSON

"Veterinarian Success Blueprint: Achieve Fast Results with Proven Strategies"

Boost Your Practice's Value, lead a High-Performance Team, Make Savvy Investment Choices, and Select the Ideal Successor

Copyright © 2024 by Mike Johnson

All rights reserved. No part of this publication may be reproduced, stored or transmitted in any form or by any means, electronic, mechanical, photocopying, recording, scanning, or otherwise without written permission from the publisher. It is illegal to copy this book, post it to a website, or distribute it by any other means without permission.

First edition

This book was professionally typeset on Reedsy. Find out more at reedsy.com

"Thinking is the hardest work there is which is probably the reason so few people engage in it."
Henry Ford

"Blessed are those who find wisdom, those who gain understanding, for she is more profitable than silver and yields better returns than gold."
Proverbs 3:13-14

Contents

Acknowledgments		ii
1	Unleashing the Power of Your Veterinary Practice and Me	1
2	Embracing the Future- AI & Business Operating System Synergy	6
3	Leading The Millenial Wave, Continuous Growth,...	10
4	Leveraging Operating Systems With AI, Synergy For the Future	21
5	A-Players, Developing and Retaining Talent	29
6	The Power of a "Next Gen Engaged Culture" and How To Get It	33
7	Leveraging Good Coaching for Enhanced Performance	38
8	Assessing Your Practice's Worth In the Market	42
9	Charting a Path to Future Success	47
10	Conclusion Story & Contact information	49

Acknowledgments

I want to thank Dr. Clark Barshinger and Tony Orsini. Two great friends, mentors and colleagues. Tony founded his company, with a card table and fold out chair, and grew Orsini Healthcare to a $500 million dollar business. He was my first CEO Round table member and client. He is a great friend to this day.

Clark and I met when he came to one of my investment banking functions and became a client. His wisdom and life's work have impacted the lives of many for the better. Especially me. He continues to be my mentor, coach and friend after 24 years. Clark Barshinger is the founder and CEO of Cherry Hill Counseling centers and has over 50 clinicians in the Chicago land area with multiple offices.

I also want to thank Bill George. He was CEO of Medtronic at the time, 2001, and I saw him speak at the Global Leadership Summit about a new type of Master's program. It was based on Emotional intelligence and your true leadership talents. He was incubating the program at Bethel college in the Minneapolis area. That is where Medtronic is located and the company he was CEO of from 1991 to 2001. As I heard him speak, I knew I had to get into that program. I did and got my Masters in Transformational leadership in 2008. Forever grateful to Bill.

Bill George is now an executive fellow at Harvard Business School, where he has been a Professor of Management Practice and Senior Fellow teaching leadership since 2004.

I am also grateful to the following authors and business coaches for their insights and wisdom, which have shaped my approach and understanding. I encourage you to explore their works and consider adding them to your library, as they have been instrumental in my own development:

- *Great By Choice* by Jim Collins
- *Investor's Business Daily*
- *True North: Discover Your Authentic Leadership,* by Bill George
- *The Seven Habits of Highly Effective People* by Stephen R. Covey
- *The Speed of Trust* by Stephen M.R. Covey
- *The Advantage* by Patrick Lencioni
- *The Five Dysfunctions of a Team* by Patrick Lencioni
- *Crucial Conversations* by Joseph Grenny, Kerry Patterson, Ron McMillan, Al Switzler, and Emily Gregory
- *Death by Meeting* by Patrick Lencioni
- *Scaling Up* by Verne Harnish
- *Traction* by Gino Wickman
- *What the Heck is EOS* by Gino Wickman and Tom Bouwer
- *Strengths Based Leadership* by Tom Rath and Barry Conchie
- *Earn It* by Jill E. Young
- *Start With Why* by Simon Sinek
- *Lessons For Living: What Only Adversity Can Teach You* by Phil Stutz
- *The Tools: 5 Tools to Help You Find Courage, Creativity, and Willpower—and Inspire You to Live Your Life in Forward Motion* by Phil Stutz and Barry Michels

Thank you to these authors for their dedication to knowledge and growth. Your work continues to enlighten and guide leaders across the globe.

1

Unleashing the Power of Your Veterinary Practice and Me

Welcome to a transformational journey tailored for a veterinarian's practice. Over the past seven years, I've had the privilege of working closely with veterinary practices and 24/7 veterinary hospitals, guiding them not just towards financial growth but also towards building confident, problem-solving leadership teams. The *Big AHA discovery* along the way: *There are **2 distinct sides to any great practice, the medical side and the business side. They both must be great! Let me repeat that, they both must be great!*** When these 2 sides of the business are synergistic. It is a beautiful thing. Heaven's part and angels sing. Everybody wins, your staff, clients, families of staff, community.

When you fight it or do not believe what I am saying your practice will struggle.

Let me explain. First, I have great respect for veterinarians. They have to go through 4 years of college undergraduate work. Then 4 more years of veterinary school to become a Doctor of Veterinary medicine. If they want to specialize, 3 to 4 more years of residency training. Lots of money and time invested. **The Point:** *They are already very good* *at being doctors and taking care of pets.* **The challenge:** *They get very little business training on how to run a successful business.* The business of running a veterinary practice, can make the doctor's life very rewarding or a bit challenging. It is everything from when the client drives onto the parking lot, enters the foyer, how they are greeted, how the office smells, time spent with the doctor and technician, and each step in between. Then the customer says thank you to the doctor and pays the bill for services rendered. So I hope you are starting to understand the Big Picture. **The client spends about 25% of their time with the doctor! The rest, 75%, is all a function of business and the people running that part of the business.** The way the business side of the practice runs has a great deal to do with how successful the Dr and all his staff will be, as well as their quality of life. I could easily list 100 things here but I will let the rest of the book do the talking. Back to my earlier point: The Dr side of the business and the business side must both be great. Seeing the big picture a little clearer? That's why this little book teaches about the key elements of what make a practice great on the business side. I know the doctors do their best to deliver great medical care. Let's deliver great business solutions to the same extent the doctors are passionate about their patient's solutions!

So to address the business side of the practice. Let me explain a little bit about myself and how I approach this. **First**, I am a business guy. I love business and my whole life has been about helping people build great businesses. My training and all my businesses have been about helping business owners build great businesses, have great careers and see the full spectrum of what a great business really looks like. **Second**, I'm also an investment banker. I understand what drives value in a business, what customers want and what investors and Private equity buyers want when they buy a business. A Veterinary practice is an asset, that is way more valuable than any DVM's 401K. How they care for and treat that asset is paramount.

This book is about the 7 big business disciplines we installed into our DVM(Doctors in Veterinary medicine) hospital leadership teams and our DVM practice leadership teams and exploded the growth of these businesses. **We grew the business 10-fold! Yes, that is 1000% over a 6-year period**. They are well positioned to take full advantage of this new wave of AI growth that is coming like a *new high-speed train*.

We didn't discover or invent any new breakthrough. What we did was focus, prioritize and build a system that delivers the **3 most important things every person desires combined with the 6 high priority, high payoff processes that guarantee these 3 great outcomes.**

1. **Security and Stability:**

o This includes financial security, job stability, and a safe living environment. They provide the foundation upon which people can build their lives, *reducing stress and allowing them to focus on growth and personal development.*

2. **Connection:**

o Whether it's through family, friendships, workplace or community, meaningful relationships provide emotional support and enrich our lives. This connection *nurtures our emotional well-being and helps us to thrive.*

3. **Purpose:**

o Having a sense of purpose and finding meaning in what we do motivates and inspires us. It can be found in our work, personal achievements, or contributions to society, and it ***drives passion and fulfillment.***

These elements are interconnected and contribute significantly to overall life satisfaction and personal fulfillment. They **resonate across various cultures and demographics, making them universally important in shaping human behavior and well-being.**

Together, we've tackled everyday challenges and recurring issues practices face. *These teams are now equipped to embrace the future of veterinary medicine, ready to capitalize on rapidly advancing technologies that smaller practices might struggle to adopt.*

In this book, I present practical strategies and actionable steps that you can apply immediately. These steps are designed to **deliver an** *excellent return on your time and investment, helping you* **effectively integrate a business operating system that fosters prioritization, communication, and collaboration.* We focus on setting and achieving structured goals** across various time-frames—from 90 days to ten years—with the core practice of weekly opportunity and obstacle meetings. These sessions **address operational challenges, enhance accountability, and create a forum for open feedback and strategic adjustments.** The result? *A more efficient practice flow, a stronger team spirit, and significant financial growth—potentially adding substantial value to your practice over time.*

As AI and new business operating systems continue to evolve, integrating these advancements will be critical. **Clients will notice** and prefer *practices that adapt quickly, securing your competitive edge.* Profit remains vital, as it supports staff, enables equipment upgrades, and enhances client satisfaction. By involving your team in understanding key financial metrics, you'll drive meaningful engagement, accountability, and a shared vision of success.

About Me: A Journey of Leadership and Growth

With a background as both an **investment banker and business coach,** I offer a unique perspective. Over the past 30 years, I've assisted businesses in navigating issues related to finance, leadership, accountability, and culture. My comprehensive approach ensures a focus on a*chieving the best return on investment, balancing time and resources wisely; while guiding individuals to work they love, alongside people they respect, with an inspiring plan & purpose.*

This book distills decades of financial and leadership knowledge into actionable steps. My philosophy, shaped by learning from mistakes, is: **"We don't win or lose; we win or learn."**

My passion has always been maximizing performance within business frameworks. I assist in aligning natural strengths with roles individuals love and excel in. Returning to college in 2005, I earned a **Master's in Transformational Leadership** from Bethel College. This program, inspired by Bill George, CEO of Medtronic, emphasized emotional intelligence for leadership, advocating vulnerability to foster collaboration, creativity, and excellence. It also exposed us to the power of a business operating systems that allow us to maximize the potential of the people that work with us.

Beginning in 2017, my journey with these veterinary groups has been both enlightening and rewarding, yielding insights now ready to share. This book offers you the *tools to maximize your practice's potential, ensuring it thrives through inevitable changes.* Join me as we explore **strategies for collaboration, strategic planning, and culture building, poised to unleash your practice's fullest potential.**

2

Embracing the Future- AI & Business Operating System Synergy

In an era of rapid technological advancement, embracing the future of veterinary practice, especially through AI readiness, is crucial. **AI integration marks a significant technological evolution**, and veterinary practices must adapt quickly to harness its potential. They must also understand and integrate a business operating system because the 2 work in synergy together. One without the other and you will only harness maybe 1/3 of what AI can bring.

Understanding Business Operating Systems

As Tom Bouwer articulates in "What the Heck is EOS?", **every business relies on some form of operating system**, though it often remains undefined. A critical challenge is that many companies struggle to understand or implement the system effectively because **leadership teams lack consistency in applying disciplined processes.**

Consequences of Inconsistency:

Poor Communication: Inconsistent application of the operating system leads to breakdowns in communication, resulting in misunderstandings.

Dysfunction: Without a uniform approach, businesses often face operational dysfunction, making it difficult for teams to work cohesively.

Frustration and Confusion: Employees become frustrated and confused about priorities, as there is no consistent framework to guide their actions.

Unrealized Potential: Ultimately, the business fails to achieve its full potential due to these alignment issues.

The Good News:

Effective operating systems such as EOS, Pinnacle, and Bloom Growth have emerged, offering structured methodologies that enhance clarity and team alignment. By implementing these systems, practices align resources and strategies, steering towards success. Over 120,000 small businesses have excelled by integrating such systems, highlighting their transformative potential.

Maximizing Practice Potential:

Adopting a structured operating system can vastly improve the functionality of veterinary practices. By leveraging these frameworks, practices position themselves to efficiently integrate AI advancements and thrive amidst rapid technological change.

The Dawn of AI in Veterinary Medicine

Revolutionizing Veterinary Practices. Fortunately we are only in the 3rd inning rounding into the 4th with AI and many practices stand poised to reap great benefits!

AI is increasingly integral to veterinary medicine, transforming patient care and management through:

Enhanced Diagnostics: AI offers rapid, accurate interpretations of X-rays and MRIs, aiding quick and precise veterinary diagnoses.

Predictive Health Monitoring: AI analyzes health data patterns for disease prediction, enabling proactive health interventions.

Telemedicine: AI-facilitated telemedicine expands veterinary care access, particularly in underserved areas.

Operational Efficiency: Automating routine administrative tasks like scheduling and billing, AI frees vets to focus on patient care.

To fully benefit, practices must maintain a structured system to integrate these technological innovations effectively.

Importance of a Certified Business Operating System:

Operating systems like EOS, Pinnacle, Bloom Browth or a customized system built for your practice by a professional coach with expertise here, provide essential consistency, helping veterinary practices overcome common pitfalls:

Clarity and Alignment: Consistency in vision and goals ensures alignment across the team.

Improved Communication: Standardized communication practices minimize confusion and enhance team cohesiveness.

Structured Problem-Solving: A systematic framework for addressing issues supports continuous improvement.

Team Health and Morale: Clarified roles and direction boost team morale and support strategic growth.

By adopting such systems, practices can fully exploit AI's potential, translating advancements into enhanced patient care, improved operations, and sustained growth.

Actionable Steps and Projected ROI:

Implement AI Tools:

Action: There are some recent AI applications that are already enhancing practices substantially. For now, simply equip staff with the AI app like Chat GPT to explore AI's role in their tasks. Let your staff ask Chat some simple questions, Like "I am a Customer service rep in a veterinary practice, Do you have some ideas that can help me be more efficient?" I asked ChatGPT that question and it gave 7 things you could do and specific strategies to help. Let each department ask ChatGPT questions and simply have a meeting to hear all the new ideas they came up with! There you will find some low hanging fruit that can be installed instantly and reap immediate returns! The neat thing about AI, it really wants to help!

Projected ROI: Implementing these simple AI suggestions can save practices approximately $20k to $50k annually through efficiency improvements, other applications substantially more!

2. Engage a Business Coach:

Action: Seek out a coach experienced with EOS, Bloom Growth, or Pinnacle to drive strategic practice improvements and financial acumen. A good coach will ask you good questions to foster big picture thinking on potential for your business. I've utilized and installed all 3 of the above systems.

Projected ROI: An experienced coach can potentially add $$$millions to business value over its life cycle by enhancing strategic thinking and operations.

3. Evaluate Practice Attractiveness:

Action: Reflect on your practice's market readiness. Consider its turnkey nature and potential attractiveness to buyers. A good business coach will have a good process to evaluate your business's valuation and tips to add value.

Projected ROI: Enhancing business attractiveness can significantly increase its market value by 20% to 50%. More on this in an upcoming chapter.

These steps can free up time, increase revenue, or add more enjoyment to your life. They allow veterinary practitioners to make more informed, impactful decisions. These actions help practices not only adapt but also thrive in a rapidly evolving technological landscape.

3

Leading The Millenial Wave, Continuous Growth, Accountability = Essential Leadership Pillars

Millennials, typically defined as those born between 1981 and 1996, bring a unique set of strengths to the workplace, influenced by the era in which they grew up. Here are some key attributes that research and studies have identified, making millennials great workers:

1. **Tech-Savvy**: Growing up in an age of rapid technological advances, millennials naturally gravitate towards digital solutions and are adept at using technology to improve efficiency and productivity in the workplace.
2. **Value-Driven**: This generation places a high value on working for companies with missions and values that align with their own. They seek roles that provide purpose and meaning, leading to high levels of engagement when these align.
3. **Collaborative Nature**: Millennials thrive in team-oriented environments. They prefer open communication and collaboration,

often resulting in innovative solutions and improved team dynamics.
4. **Adaptability**: Raised during times of significant change, millennials are generally adaptable and open to new experiences. They are comfortable with change and can handle transitions such as shifts in workplace practices or technology.
5. **Continuous Learning**: Millennials value personal growth and are eager for opportunities to develop professionally. They seek ongoing education and training, which often results in a highly skilled and evolving workforce.
6. **Work-Life Balance**: While they value hard work, millennials also prioritize a healthy work-life balance. This perspective can lead to more sustainable productivity and can help prevent burnout.
7. **Diversity and Inclusion Champions**: Millennials tend to be more open-minded and supportive of diversity and inclusion in the workplace. They strive for workplaces that are equitable and inclusive, which can foster a more harmonious and productive work environment.

These attributes demonstrate why millennials, and next gens can be exceptional contributors to any organization. Their unique approach to work prioritizes efficiency, meaning, and balance, resulting in innovative and dynamic teams. Leveraging these strengths can lead to positive outcomes for both businesses and employees alike.

Here are real-world examples that help illustrate how millennials and next gen staff excel in the workplace with their unique attributes:
1. **Tech-Savvy**:
    o **Example**: At companies like Facebook and Google, millennials lead in developing and employing cutting-edge technologies and innovations. Their familiarity with digital tools and platforms allows

them to streamline processes and enhance productivity.

o **Impact**: Their ability to adapt quickly to new technologies means they can efficiently manage remote work tools, which became crucial during the COVID-19 pandemic for maintaining business operations.

2. **Value-Driven**:

o **Example**: Companies such as Patagonia and Ben & Jerry's attract millennial workers with their focus on sustainability and social responsibility. These brands align their business operations with environmental and social values, which resonates deeply with millennial employees.

o **Impact**: This alignment can result in increased employee satisfaction and retention, as workers feel their personal values are supported by their employer.

3. **Collaborative Nature**:

o **Example**: At tech companies like Slack, the emphasis on teamwork and communication tools reflects the millennial penchant for collaboration. These environments are designed to foster open communication and teamwork, allowing for more creative problem-solving.

o **Impact**: Millennials' preference for collaboration often leads to a more inclusive approach to projects, gathering diverse perspectives that can drive innovation.

4. **Adaptability**:

o **Example**: Startups and fast-paced industries like fintech benefit from millennials' adaptability. Companies such as Square have thrived by leveraging young employees who can quickly adjust to industry disruptions and market changes.

o **Impact**: Their flexibility and readiness to embrace change help companies remain competitive and responsive to evolving business landscapes.

5. **Continuous Learning**:

o **Example**: LinkedIn provides extensive learning resources and encourages ongoing professional development, appealing to millennials' desire for growth. This dedication to constant learning helps employees keep skills up to date.

o **Impact**: Companies that support continuous learning see improvements in employee performance and innovation, as millennials bring fresh skills and ideas to the table.

6. **Work-Life Balance**:

o **Example**: Organizations like Dropbox have instituted flexible working hours and remote work policies, which appeal to millennials who seek work-life balance. This approach helps cater to their preference for balancing personal and professional commitments.

o **Impact**: By advocating for a balanced lifestyle, these companies often experience lower turnover rates and higher job satisfaction among employees.

7. **Diversity and Inclusion Champions**:

o **Example**: Salesforce and Microsoft are known for their strong diversity and inclusion initiatives, which attract millennials. These companies actively promote varied perspectives and backgrounds within their workforce.

o **Impact**: Millennials help foster work environments that prioritize inclusivity, leading to enhanced creativity and a wider array of innovative solutions.

By integrating these attributes and examples, organizations can harness the strengths of millennial workers to foster an agile, value-driven, and inclusive workplace that encourages growth and adaptability.

Embracing the values that millennials prioritize and **fostering a culture of continuous learning and innovative management techniques can yield significant benefits for employers. Here are some key advantages:**

1. **Enhanced Innovation and Creativity**:

- By supporting continuous learning and diverse management techniques, companies can tap into millennials' creative potential. These employees are likely to bring fresh perspectives and innovative solutions to business challenges.

2. **Increased Employee Engagement and Retention:**
   - Aligning company values with those of millennial employees fosters a sense of purpose and belonging. Engaged employees are more committed and less likely to leave, reducing turnover rates and the associated costs of hiring and training new staff.

3. **Agile and Adaptable Workforce:**
   - Encouraging constant development ensures that the workforce remains agile and responsive to market changes. This adaptability is crucial for companies operating in fast-paced industries where innovation dictates success.

4. **Improved Organizational Culture:**
   - Emphasizing values such as work-life balance, inclusivity, and continuous growth helps create a positive organizational culture. Such environments attract top talent and facilitate a collaborative atmosphere where all employees can thrive.

5. **Stronger Brand Reputation:**
   - Companies that embody progressive and inclusive practices build a strong brand reputation. This public image can attract more customers, partners, and top-notch talent, further enhancing the company's competitive edge.

6. **Better Problem-Solving and Decision-Making:**
   - A workforce that is continuously learning brings new skills and perspectives to the table. This diversity of thought leads to better problem-solving strategies and more informed decision-making processes.

7. **Increased Productivity and Efficiency:**
   - Engaged employees who are continually learning and applying new techniques are generally more productive. They contribute to

more efficient workflows and processes, thereby improving the overall performance of the organization.

8. **Alignment with Future Trends**:

o By adopting values aligned with millennial priorities, companies position themselves to seamlessly integrate future workplace trends, maintaining relevance and competitiveness in an ever-evolving market.

By leveraging these benefits, employers not only **secure the loyalty and productivity of their millennial workforce but also enhance their overall business performance** and sustainability. This win-win scenario ensures that both employees and employers thrive in a dynamic and challenging business environment.

Investing in the career development of millennial staff can lead to several monetary benefits for organizations. Here are some of the financial advantages:

1. **Reduced Turnover Costs**:

o High employee turnover is costly, factoring in recruitment, training, and lost productivity. By fostering career development, companies can enhance employee satisfaction and loyalty, significantly reducing turnover rates and the associated costs.

2. **Increased Productivity and Efficiency**:

o Career development programs equip employees with new skills and knowledge, leading to improved productivity and efficiency. This increase in workplace efficiency can have a direct positive impact on the company's bottom line.

3. **Higher Employee Engagement**:

o Engaged employees often perform better, contributing to higher revenue per employee. Career development opportunities can boost engagement levels, translating to increased performance and profitability.

4. **Innovation and Competitive Edge**:

o By encouraging learning and development, companies often spur innovation. Employees who are skilled and knowledgeable will drive innovative projects that can open new revenue streams and provide a competitive advantage in the market.

5. **Enhanced Reputation and Attraction of Talent:**

o Companies known for investing in employee development often attract top talent, reducing recruitment costs. A strong reputation as a learning organization can negate the need for expensive recruitment drives and increase the quality of applicants.

6. **Better Customer Service and Satisfaction:**

o Well-developed employees tend to deliver superior customer service, enhancing customer satisfaction and loyalty. Happy customers are more likely to return and recommend the business, leading to increased sales.

7. **Efficiency in Adapting to Market Changes:**

o Skilled employees can quickly adapt to new technologies and processes, minimizing downtime and retraining costs. This agility enables businesses to respond swiftly to market demands, maintaining or increasing market share.

8. **Cultivation of Future Leaders:**

o Investing in talent development helps identify and prepare future leaders within the organization, reducing the need for costly external hires. Promoting internally can save on recruitment and onboarding costs, while also retaining valuable organizational knowledge.

By focusing on your next gens career development, companies not only foster a more engaged and productive workforce but also realize tangible financial benefits that contribute to long-term business success.

What role does accountability play in promoting a healthy culture and fostering career growth in our next gen employees?

Accountability plays a crucial role in fostering a healthy organizational culture and supporting career growth, especially for next-generation employees like millennials and Gen Z. Here's **how accountability contributes** to these aspects:

1. **Enhances Trust and Transparency**:

o When accountability is ingrained in the culture, it fosters a transparent environment where employees trust leadership and each other. This transparency builds a strong foundation for open communication, crucial for a healthy workplace culture.

2. **Empowers Employees**:

o *By holding employees accountable, organizations empower them to take ownership of their roles and responsibilities.* This empowerment leads to increased confidence and encourages proactive contributions, which aids in personal and professional growth.

3. **Drives Performance**:

o Accountability *ensures that employees are aware of their goals and how their actions impact the organization. This awareness motivates them to perform better a*nd strive for excellence, which can lead to career advancements.

4. **Encourages Responsibility**:

o When employees know they are accountable for their outcomes, they are *more likely to act responsibly and make informed decisions. This sense of responsibility promotes maturity and professional development.*

5. **Facilitates Feedback and Improvement**:

o Regularly assessing performance and holding individuals accountable allows for *constructive feedback. This feedback is essential for individual growth as it highlights areas of improvement and encourages ongoing learning.*

6. **Promotes Teamwork and Collaboration**:

o Accountability in team settings **enhances collaboration as team members** rely on each other to meet shared objectives. This strengthens teamwork and builds a supportive environment conducive to collective and individual success.

7. **Aligns Personal and Organizational Goals**:

o Holding employees accountable a*ligns their personal career progression with organizational objectives, creating a win-win situation.* Employees are more motivated to achieve their personal goals when they see how they contribute to the organization's success.

8. **Encourages Goal Setting**:

o Accountability encourages clear *goal setting, both personally and professionally. By setting and evaluating goals, employees can track their progress and take ownership of their career paths, while also driving company success.*

Incorporating a culture of accountability nurtures an environment where next-gen employees can thrive and develop their careers. It ensures that individuals feel valued and challenged, which helps in retaining talented employees and building a strong, dynamic workforce.

Can a veterinary practice with 2 DVM's, 3 techs, 2 assistants and 2 CSR's implement many of the advantages mentioned previously? Here's how your practice can benefit and the potential financial implications:

Implementation in a Small Veterinary Practice:

1. **Tech-Savvy Operations**:

o **Strategy**: Leverage technology for scheduling, patient records, and diagnostics. Use AI tools for routine procedures such as appointment bookings and reminders.

o **Financial Implication**: While there's an initial investment in technology, you'll benefit from reduced administrative costs and improved efficiency long-term. It can also enhance client satisfaction, potentially increasing repeat visits.

2. **Value-Driven Culture:**

o **Strategy**: Emphasize a mission of compassionate, high-quality care for animals. Align practice policies and procedures with these values.

o **Financial Implication**: A strong value-driven culture boosts staff satisfaction and retention, reducing the costly turnover that can disrupt operations and impact service quality.

3. **Collaborative Environment**:

o **Strategy**: Encourage open communication among team members through regular meetings and collaborative case reviews.

o **Financial Implication**: Improved teamwork can lead to more efficient problem-solving, reducing time wasted during consultations and enhancing overall service quality, which in turn can increase client loyalty and revenue.

4. **Adaptable Practices**:

o **Strategy**: Implement flexible protocols to swiftly adapt to new medical practices or technology.

o **Financial Implication**: Adaptability reduces downtime and ensures your practice remains competitive, capturing new clients and services without needing extensive retraining or resources.

5. **Continuous Learning**:

o **Strategy**: Invest in ongoing training and development for team members to keep their skills current.

o **Financial Implication**: Training incurs costs but yields a highly competent workforce that can perform a wider range of services. This can improve service offerings, leading to increased client satisfaction and revenue.

6. **Work-Life Balance**:

o **Strategy**: Offer flexible working hours and ensure workloads are manageable to prevent burnout.

o **Financial Implication**: While scheduling may be complex, maintaining balanced workloads reduces burnout-related absenteeism and turnover, both of which are costly to replace.

7. **Diversity and Inclusion**:

o **Strategy**: Foster an inclusive work environment where all employees feel valued and respected.

o **Financial Implication**: An inclusive environment can improve employee morale and satisfaction, reducing turnover costs and enhancing productivity.

Financial Implications:

- **Initial Costs**: Investment in technology and employee training will be the most immediate financial requirements. However, these should be viewed as strategic investments that enhance operational efficiency and service quality.
- **Long-term Savings**: Improved employee retention and productivity will lead to significant cost savings. Enhanced operational efficiency can reduce overtime and eliminate redundant tasks.
- **Revenue Growth**: By offering superior service and maintaining high client satisfaction, your practice can increase client retention and attract new clients through referrals.
- **Competitive Edge**: *Practices that embrace these principles may find additional revenue streams as they attract clientele seeking cutting-edge veterinary care distinguished by excellent service and personal attention.*

In summary, understand that Next Gens need to be challenged and be in a career growth, business growth environment or they get restless and look for the next challenge. Implementing these strategies requires thoughtful investment, but **the long-term gains in efficiency, employee satisfaction, and client loyalty can offset these costs, ultimately benefiting the financial health of your practice. These gains would also be a part of a good Business Operating System.**

4

Leveraging Operating Systems With AI, Synergy For the Future

Ok, quick point to make here. I am a member of the Baby boomer generation. We are not the brightest bulbs in the closet when it comes to technology. I am not a guru of technology, but I do have a certain amount of common sense and I've seen enough technological advances to realize this one is going to be a good one. It will make life easier for a lot of people, especially in the medical and veterinary space. Probably, the key point to understand is your customers are using AI. In April of this year the Chat GPT app had nearly 2 billion visits. So, our customers will start expecting their veterinary practices to have it. This is one of those movements that is going to make us adapt quickly or we will have to understand we could lose business to those that have already adapted.

The insights I provided are based on common trends and applications of AI in veterinary medicine as acknowledged in industry discussions and publications. Here are a few examples from the industry where AI is making an impact in 6 different companies.

1. **VetCT**: This company uses AI to aid radiologists by providing advanced imaging solutions, which help in diagnosing conditions more accurately and efficiently.
2. **Idexx Laboratories**: They employ AI to enhance their diagnostic tools, allowing for quicker analysis of lab tests and imaging results for better patient management.
3. **TeleVet and Airvet**: Platforms like these leverage AI to improve telemedicine services, facilitating remote consultations that are more convenient and accessible for pet owners.
4. **Petuum and One Health**: These companies work on AI systems that integrate data from various sources to predict health trends and outbreaks, aiding in timely preventive measures in veterinary practices.

These represent actual implementations and the growing role of AI in the veterinary industry.

Key Points on AI in Veterinary Medicine

1. **Enhanced Diagnostics**: AI algorithms can analyze X-rays, ultrasounds, and pathology slides with greater speed and accuracy than traditional methods, aiding veterinarians in diagnosing conditions more reliably.
2. **Predictive Analytics**: By analyzing historical data, AI can predict outbreaks of diseases, helping in early intervention and preventive care measures which can improve animal health outcomes.
3. **Automated Operations**: AI-driven software can manage routine administrative tasks like scheduling, reminders, and record-keeping, allowing veterinary staff to focus on patient care and reducing human error.
4. **Improved Client Communication**: AI tools can facilitate better communication with pet owners through personalized updates

and education on pet care, increasing client engagement and satisfaction.
5. **Cost Efficiency**: Implementing AI can reduce costs associated with diagnostic errors and operational inefficiencies, leading to savings that can be reinvested in the practice for better equipment or higher wages.
6. **Telemedicine**: AI enables more effective telemedicine consultations, which can expand practice reach and convenience for clients who may be unable to visit in person.

Encouraging veterinary staff to explore AI applications and utilize them to seek interactive and practical solutions for everyday challenges can lead to substantial improvements in practice operations. *By starting small, such as using AI for scheduling or initial diagnostics, and gradually incorporating more advanced tools, the veterinary staff can experience firsthand the transformative effects of AI in their work environmen*t.

Here are the benefits to a practice from having an **up-to-date technology with the human side of the business, meaning a system for organizing our human energy,** combined with the potential that AI is offering. *So here is the* **key point** *I believe I am driving home here.* I hope so. The human side of the business is very special and precious. Hopefully we do not have a future that is all robots and AI. Our fellow workers are key. Yes, we all have flaws, but it is in the cooperation, the team work, collaboration, the team planning, building purpose and values into the business, the prioritizing, the roles clarification, leading and managing, the day to day living and working together is where the beauty lies! This is what a good operating system helps you and your team accomplish.

It is through these types of tools and good coaching, that **we are shaped and molded into better people.** Better friends, better teammates, better spouses, better parents. This is the beauty of teams! Good teams shape us and mold us into better versions of ourselves. They are truly a blessing to the people that work there and the clientele they serve. We do not have enough of these types of businesses in the world. **A good coach, good owners, team leaders, along with these 2 technologies have the potential to make an incredible impact on your team and their communities!**

Integrating AI tools with your *"Business Operating System"* like Traction, Bloom Growth or Pinnacle can create a **powerful synergy that enhances efficiency, patient care, cost savings, and revenue. Here's how they can work together:**
Synergistic Benefits
1. Enhanced Operational Efficiency

- **BOS Framework**: Provides a structured approach to organizing the practice, with defined roles, clear goals, and accountability processes. This creates a more disciplined approach to managing tasks and meeting objectives.
- **AI Automation**: Handles repetitive tasks such as scheduling, reminders, and patient follow-ups, reducing the workload on staff and minimizing human error. This allows the team to focus on strategic and patient care activities outlined by your BOS.

2. Improved Patient Care

- **BOS Clarity**: Ensures that everyone is aligned with the practice's mission and patient care goals, enhancing teamwork and patient interaction.
- **AI Diagnostics and Monitoring**: Uses advanced analytics to improve accuracy and speed of diagnoses, providing better outcomes for patients. AI can also monitor patient data continuously, alerting

staff to issues proactively.

3. Cost Savings

- **BOS Financial Management**: Offers systems for tracking financial metrics closely, identifying inefficiencies, and ensuring optimal resource allocation.
- **AI Cost Efficiency**: Reduces operational costs by streamlining processes, improving inventory management, and reducing diagnostic errors—all of which contribute to financial savings.

4. Increased Revenue

- **BOS Growth Strategies**: Establishes clear pathways for growth, keeping the team focused on expanding services and improving client retention.
- **AI Upselling and Cross-Selling**: Analyzes client data to identify opportunities for offering additional services or products, enhancing revenue per client.

Implementation Approach

1. **Strategic Planning**: Use BOS to define strategic objectives and incorporate AI tools to meet these objectives efficiently.
2. **Process Integration**: Implement AI solutions that align with your BOS-defined processes for scheduling, financial management, and client communication.
3. **Continuous Improvement**: Leverage AI analytics to provide insights and feedback on operations, allowing the BOS framework to adapt and refine processes for continuous improvement.
4. **Training and Culture**: Cultivate a culture of learning where

staff understands both the BOS methodology and AI applications, encouraging innovation and agile responses to challenges.

By combining the strategic framework and discipline of BOS with the cutting-edge capabilities of AI, your veterinary practice can operate more effectively, deliver superior patient care, realize significant cost savings, and drive revenue growth, all while fostering a supportive and innovative workplace environment. ☆

The results of the synergistic combination of these 2 systems:

Integrating AI tools and an operating system like Bloom Growth can significantly *enhance the culture of a veterinary practice by fostering a more empowered, efficient, and collaborative environment. Here's how* **solving problems faster** *can positively impact practice culture*:

1. Empowerment and Confidence

- **Rapid Problem-Solving**: When issues are resolved quickly, staff members feel more capable and empowered in their roles. This boost in confidence encourages them to take initiative and make proactive decisions.
- **Skill Development**: As staff engage with AI technologies and strategic frameworks, they acquire new skills and knowledge, which increases their sense of value and professional growth.

2. Collaboration and Teamwork

- **Aligned Goals**: BOS helps create a clear vision and shared goals, which unites the team around common objectives, improving collaboration.
- **Enhanced Communication**: With AI handling routine tasks and providing insights, team members have more time to communicate

effectively and work collaboratively on complex issues.

3. Efficiency and Focus

- **Less Stress**: Automating routine tasks reduces workload pressure, leading to less stress and a more positive work environment.
- **Focus on Value-adding Activities**: Freed from mundane tasks, staff can focus on higher-value activities, such as patient care or client interaction, which are more rewarding and fulfilling.

4. Innovation and Adaptability

- **Culture of Innovation**: Regular interaction with AI systems encourages a mindset of continuous improvement and learning, promoting an innovative culture.
- **Agility**: By solving problems faster, the practice becomes more adaptable to changes and challenges, making the team resilient and open to new opportunities.

5. Job Satisfaction and Retention

- **Increased Satisfaction**: A supportive culture that embraces efficient problem-solving reduces frustration and boosts job satisfaction.
- **Higher Retention Rates**: Happy and engaged employees are more likely to stay, reducing turnover and fostering long-term team cohesion.

By streamlining problem-solving and enhancing operational efficiencies, AI and a strong operating system, together, contribute to a positive, innovative, and adaptable workplace culture. This

not only improves daily operations but also elevates overall job satisfaction, making the practice a more attractive place to work for current and future staff members. ✯You are probably starting to see how this combination of systems can exponentially advance a practice's morale, profits and fun. Give me a call so we can discuss installing a program like this into your practice. (847)-372-3432.

5

A-Players, Developing and Retaining Talent

"*Sometimes it's easier to change people than to change the people.*"
- Greg Clery

"To significantly increase your revenue and profit, start by elevating your leadership team."

You might not always recognize if you have the wrong people on your team. They may seem suitable until you bring in a few A-players, and the difference becomes evident. These A-players might not have the most industry experience or the perfect academic background, but their presence is transformative. For example, one client's company experienced unprecedented growth with a new team, allowing the owner to enjoy family vacations, even during peak seasons. This transformation was sparked by creating a cohesive leadership team of A-players. Focusing on securing A-players can be a game-changer. Assess your leadership team: Who might be in the wrong seat?

Empower A-Players
Once you hire A-players, allow them the freedom to excel. Provide

them with ample space to lead, and they will tackle significant challenges and drive success. Generously investing in them is crucial, as the ROI of an A-player is consistently worthwhile. Their impact is immediate, often beginning on day one.

Nurturing and Retaining A-Players

Adopt structured approaches inspired by leadership and talent management strategies to develop and retain A-players. Here's how:

1. **Develop A-Players:**

o **Talent Identification**: Regularly evaluate performance to identify those with high potential who exceed expectations and exhibit leadership qualities.

o **Personal Development Plans**: Customize development plans to enhance individual strengths and align with their career aspirations, offering avenues for skill development and leadership roles.

2. **Provide Growth Opportunities:**

o **Mentorship and Coaching**: Establish mentorship programs for A-players to exchange roles as mentors and mentees, facilitating learning and leadership.

o **Challenging Assignments**: Give projects that challenge their abilities, encouraging innovation and skill demonstration.

3. **Recognition and Rewards:**

o **Public Acknowledgment**: Regularly recognize their contributions in meetings or newsletters, ensuring they feel valued and seen.

o **Performance-Based Incentives**: Offer bonuses, promotions, or special opportunities to motivate continuous excellence.

Key-Understanding A-Player Needs:

1. **Feedback and Involvement**:

o Regularly provide feedback and involve A-players in strategic discussions to align their goals with the organization's goals.

2. **Career Advancement**:

o Clearly outline career paths and provide leadership development programs to prepare them for higher responsibilities.

3. **Work-Life Balance**:

o Offer flexible work arrangements, ensuring a healthy work-life balance which is crucial for engagement.

4. **Impactful Work**:

o Ensure roles have a clear purpose and impact, making their work more meaningful and satisfying.

By strategically developing and addressing the needs of A-players, veterinary practices can cultivate an environment where talent thrives and contributes their best efforts to the organization's success. Additionally, for engaging young talent, focus on promoting a dynamic and inclusive culture while ensuring meaningful, flexible work experiences.

Here are *three action steps and examples of potential returns on investment, time, and cultural contributions* when focusing on nurturing, attracting, and retaining A-Players in your veterinary practice:

Action Steps

1. **Conduct Regular Talent Audits:**

o Evaluate your team regularly to identify high-potential employees. Use performance metrics and leadership assessments to ensure you have the right people in the right roles.

2. **Implement a Comprehensive Mentorship Program:**

o Establish programs that pair A-players with both new hires and seasoned employees. This can help share knowledge, encourage leadership development, and foster a learning culture within your practice.

3. **Offer Competitive Compensation and Flexible Work Arrangements:**

o Ensure your compensation packages are competitive and align with industry standards. Additionally, provide options for flexible work hours or remote work, which can increase job satisfaction and retain top talent.

Potential ROI Examples

1. **Return on Investment (ROI):**

o By investing in high-quality professional development and leadership training, you can reduce turnover and lower the costs associated with hiring and training new employees. High-performing A-players can boost revenue growth through enhanced client service and innovation in practice operations.

2. **Return on Time:**

o A cohesive team of A-players can streamline processes, enhance efficiency, and reduce the time spent on problem-solving. This allows you to focus on strategic business initiatives rather than day-to-day operational challenges.

3. **Return on Culture:**

o Cultivating a team of A-players can enhance your practice's culture by fostering an environment of excellence, collaboration, and innovation. This positive culture not only attracts top talent but also improves client satisfaction and loyalty, as employees are more engaged and motivated.

o **Implementing these strategies can significantly impact your veterinary practice's success, providing tangible benefits in terms of financial performance, operational efficiency, and organizational culture.**

6

The Power of a "Next Gen Engaged Culture" and How To Get It

Lena, the leader of a bustling veterinary hospital, was known for her kindness, patience, and big heart. Her vision was clear: to embed the Big Three deliverables—Security and Stability, Meaning and Purpose, Love and Connection—within her hospital staff. With a strong desire to foster a nurturing environment, Lena sought to transform the hospital's culture and aligned with a coaching process to achieve this.

Coaching Process:

Together, we embarked on a journey to instill **a disciplined meeting cadence, crucial to cultivating a strong, healthy culture**. Our approach emphasized creating a **safe, collaborative space where team members could openly share obstacles and opportunities, achieving growth both individually and collectively.**

A key component of this transformation was **taking the leadership team away for two, one-day retreat sessions.** These retreats provided the necessary environment for deep reflection and strategic planning, where **the leadership team of the hospital discerned and committed to live by values that resonated deeply with their** mission: Teamwork, Passion for Excellence, Compassionate Care, and Trusted Partnerships. These values became the foundation for their culture. They also collaborated on their long term vision and goals for the hospital. This new Vision, Goals and Values guided all subsequent decisions and actions.

Here is the structure of the staff meetings used to assure accountability to goals.

The meeting cadence included:

- **Daily Huddles (10 minutes):** Quick check-ins to address immediate issues, what we learned yesterday and align today's priorities.
- **Weekly Opportunities & Obstacles Meeting (60 minutes):** This pivotal meeting accelerates efficiency by addressing hurdles and seizing new opportunities, fostering fluidity, joy, and growth.

Meeting Structure:

1. **Check-in (5 minutes):** Team members share recent positive experiences, fostering a positive atmosphere.
2. **90-Day Goal Progress (5 minutes):** Updates on quarterly goals ensure accountability, moving unresolved challenges to the Obstacle and Opportunity (O/O) box for solution.
3. **Weekly Data Points or KPIs (5 minutes):** Reviewing key metrics allows the team to gauge progress and impact.
4. **Headlines (5 minutes):** Share important updates, both for the team and clients, ensuring awareness and engagement.
5. **To-Dos Completion (5 minutes):** Accountability checks for assigned tasks, reinforcing commitment to actions.
6. **Obstacles and Opportunities (30 minutes):** Focused discussion for resolving challenges and integrating new opportunities, with actionable to-dos.

7. **Wrap-up (5 minutes):** Summarize key messages for broader staff communication and rate the meeting to ensure effectiveness and alignment.

- **Quarterly All-Day Meeting (8 hours):** Comprehensive reviews of the annual plan, revisiting values, evaluating plans, celebrating wins, learning from mistakes, and setting 90-day priorities.

Action Steps:

1. **Implement the Meeting Cadence:** Begin with establishing the daily and weekly meetings to foster a consistent rhythm and habit of accountability.
2. **Define Key Performance Indicators (KPIs):** Identify and agree on the critical metrics that align with growth and quality service goals.
3. **Assign and Track 90-Day Goals:** Clearly assign objectives linked to these KPIs and ensure regular progress checks.

Results and Benefits:

As the leadership team came together, they d**iscovered a shared ambition: to expand their 24/7/365 care into communities lacking life-saving veterinary services**. This breakthrough **underscored a universal truth—everyone has a need to grow and become the best version of themselves.** The team realized that career development pathways are vital, particularly for younger generations, who often seek continual growth and avoid roles that feel stagnating.

In today's rapidly evolving business landscape, veterinary managers and practice owners must recognize that change, accelerated by the internet and AI, is inevitable. The **younger staff, those under 40, closely observe whether businesses are keeping pace with these** changes. If not, they are likely to move to more innovative and forward-thinking environments. **This shift is also evident among customers who are increasingly adopting AI to enhance their lives.**

With this robust framework in place, Lena and her team not only cultivated a vibrant and accountable culture but also achieved remarkable success. Over four years, **the hospital experienced a remarkable 300% growth**, establishing itself as the premier 24/7 pet hospital in the area.

ROI Benefits:

1. **Increased Efficiency:** The streamlined meetings and clear action steps enabled the team to address challenges swiftly, enhancing overall productivity.
2. **High Employee Retention:** By creating clear growth pathways and ensuring team engagement, the hospital retained skilled professionals who were committed to the mission.
3. **Enhanced Client Satisfaction:** The focus on critical KPIs and seamless teamwork translated into improved client service and satisfaction, contributing to the hospital's reputation and growth.
4. **The power of these strategic retreats:** and disciplined processes showcased how a committed leadership team, supported by **shared values and a clear mission, can drive cultural transformation and achieve significant success.**

Further Reading:

For anyone interested in deepening their understanding of building a strong culture tailored for modern generations, I highly recommend "The Culture Code" by Daniel Coyle. This book provides valuable insights into the elements that make a successful team culture, offering practical ideas that can be applied to any organizational setting.

7

Leveraging Good Coaching for Enhanced Performance

Coaching and mentorship play a vital role in professional development and can significantly contribute to creating an impactful workplace culture. Here's what you need to consider about this topic:

The Role of Coaching and Mentorship
1. Empowerment Through Guidance:

- Coaching and mentorship are powerful tools for empowering individuals. They provide a platform for sharing knowledge and skills, **helping people unlock their potential and become more confident in their abilities.**

2. Creating Safe Spaces:

- Establishing an environment where employees feel safe to express themselves is crucial. These spaces allow individuals to be vulnerable, honest, and transparent, leading to genuine communication and deeper connections.

3. Encouraging Vulnerability and Transparency:

- Vulnerability is no longer seen as a weakness but rather a strength in today's evolving workplaces. It encourages open dialogue, fosters trust, and enables team members to provide and receive constructive feedback.

4. The Demand from Next-Gen Employees:

- The next generation highly values workplaces where they feel understood and supported. They look for mentors and coaches who can offer structured guidance while valuing transparency and collaborative feedback.

A Future Focused on Support: The **demand for supportive mentorship is particularly strong among the next generation of employees. They seek guidance and clarity, looking for mentors who can not only guide them in their careers** but also help them navigate their personal aspirations.

Now here is how I coach your leaders and managers to implement this.

1. **Leverage the Right Roles:**

o Ensure that the **right people are in the right seat**s within your organization. This involves assessing employees' strengths and aligning them with their roles to maximize productivity and satisfaction. I also use the Gallup organizations Strength Finder online talent assessment.

o https://www.gallup.com/cliftonstrengths/en/252137/home.aspx

o This test helps your employee, and you see what their natural born strengths are. This way you can help guide them into **their best area to succeed and make their greatest contribution** to your business.

2. **Clear Accountability:**

o Establish **clear responsibility lines** so everyone knows their duties and accountability. This promotes **ownership and efficient workflow management** in the team.

3. **Provide Regular Feedback:**

o Engage in consistent feedback loops with your team. Communication should be open, honest, and frequent to motivate employees and help them grow. Feedback is the breakfast of champions!

o I recommend a 90 day "1 on 1" with each employee. A good book for using that format is *"How to Be a Great Boss"* by Gino Wickman

4. **Foster Strong Relationships:**

o Build genuine relationships with your team members. Understanding them on a personal level strengthens mutual respect and collaboration.

5. **Use Data for Effective Management:**

o Implement metrics and KPIs as part of data-driven management to objectively measure performance and make informed decisions.

o They want to know how well they are doing. A good **scorecard and talent assessment tools** art great for creating awareness and guidance for improvement.

6. **Lead by Example:**

o Demonstrate the behavior and work ethic you expect from your team. Leading by example inspires employees and sets the standard for the organization. **During 1/1 time ask each employee how they think you are doing? What do they see that could help you do better?**

These principles are designed to help supervisors *create a productive and positive workplace culture, helping both the business and the employees to excel.*

Some companies and sports teams that lead the field with coaching and mentoring and are worth mentioning here:

San Antonio Spurs (NBA):

- The Spurs are known for their strong culture built on trust, transparency, and mutual respect. Coach Gregg Popovich emphasizes personal relationships and open communication, nurturing an environment where players feel valued and understood.

Salesforce:

- Salesforce promotes a culture of feedback through mentorship. Their V2MOM process (Vision, Values, Methods, Obstacles, and Measures) helps employees align personal and professional goals while fostering transparent communication throughout all levels of the organization.

Let's commit to creating an environment where coaching and mentorship become integral to your team culture. By doing so, you will not only achieve your collective goals but also empower each other to reach new heights of personal and professional excellence.

8

Assessing Your Practice's Worth In the Market

In the realm of veterinary practice, understanding how to navigate private equity and investment is pivotal. This chapter will empower you to **confidently evaluate the value of your practice and find the right private equity (PE) partner, ensuring your practice's success and longevity.**

Understanding Your Practice's Worth

Assessing your practice value is a crucial step when potential buyers express interest. My background as an investment banker and my credentials in Transformational Leadership and Business Operating Systems equip me to guide you in this journey. Here's what we focus on:

Questions a good buyer will ask *and questions you need to know.*

1- Are you running on a certified operating system installed by a qualified coach? How far into the organization is the system? Is every employee aware of the system and in a weekly opportunity/obstacle meeting?

2- How many competitors are there in your market?

3- How unique is your practice in the market? Is there a strong competitive advantage?

4- How functional and aligned are your leadership team? Are all leaders open and honest? Are they willing to become their best?

5- Is the business growing? At what rate? 0-100?

6- What types of regulations are attached to the business?

7- How much debt do they have? Do they need a capital infusion and how much?

8- How many DVM's are at this practice?

9- What's the current interest rate environment?

These above questions with EBITDA determine your value.

Actionable Steps and Projected ROI

1. **Implement a Certified Business Operating System:**

o **Action:** Introduce a business operating system such as EOS, Pinnacle, Bloom Growth or a customized system designed for your team by a good, experienced coach. These streamline operations and maximize efficiency. Building a more turnkey practice. Also a more liquid practice making it more attractive to potential investors/buyers.

o **Projected ROI:** A potential **increase in practice value by 25% to 100% within 12 to 18** months due to increased revenue, profit, operational efficiency, team health, consistency and accountability.

2. **Conduct a Comprehensive Market Analysis:**

o **Action:** Analyze the local market dynamics, including growth potential and competitive landscape.

o **Projected ROI:** A strategic understanding can position the business for a premium valuation, potentially increasing market value based on effective positioning and competitive differentiation.

3. **Engage Professional Guidance for Valuation:**

o **Action:** Work with financial and industry experts to accurately assess practice value and prepare for negotiations.

o **Projected ROI:** Secure a sale price 20% + above initial offers by understanding true market value and enhancing negotiation capability.

By taking these actions, you'll not only enhance the value of your practice but also ensure a smoother transition, greater financial return and produce a better list of options for you.

1. **Evaluate Options:**

o Decide whether to continue independently or partner with a PE investor.

2. **Plan Your Future:**

o Determine your retirement timeline.

o Decide whether you want to retire from practice.

o Consider enhancing your business by implementing a custom business operating system combined with advanced AI to boost team efficiency, profitability, and value. The timeline to adequately install an operating system is 18-24 months. So if you are thinking about retiring in the next 3-5 years the time to find your advocate to help you discern your best options is now.

3. **Reap the Benefits:**

o Gain flexibility in retirement, whether selling your practice for the best price or continuing to draw income while *working on your terms.*

Deciphering EBITDA

Understanding EBITDA is key to evaluating your practice's market value. EBITDA—Earnings Before Interest, Taxes, Depreciation, and Amortization—offers a clear view of operational performance, vital for comparison and valuation:

- **Operational Efficiency:** Allows for comparison across companies by removing non-operating factors.
- **Valuation Tool:** Indicates potential cash flow, essential for mergers and acquisitions.
- **Limitations:** Does not address capital expenditures or debt.

Using EBITDA alongside other metrics can provide a comprehensive financial analysis.

Ensuring a Fair Price and a Smooth Sale

To secure a good price and streamline the selling process, consider these strategies:

- **Seek Expert Guidance:** Partner with a knowledgeable mentor familiar with finance, valuations, and PE acquisitions.
- **Plan for Post-Sale:** Know what will happen to your practice and team post-purchase.
- **Understand Contracts:** Clarify responsibilities and the duration you're bound to the practice's success post-sale.

Identifying the Right PE Partner

Choosing the right PE partner is critical for your practice and employees. Here's what to expect:

- You may need to stay engaged for 1-2 years post-sale, ensuring a smooth transition.
- Be prepared for potential conflicts if your vision differs from that of the buyer.
- Understand the implications of changes imposed by the new owners.

To identify an ideal PE buyer, they should:

1. Be running on a certified business operating system like EOS, Pinnacle, or Bloom Growth.
2. Demonstrate market expertise and a commitment to sustainable growth by showcasing their track record.
3. Present a compelling vision, values, and mission that align with

your practice ethos.

If the buyer cannot demonstrate alignment with these principles, reconsider the sale, and consult with me for buyers who value this informed process. It is key to understand what the buyer brings to the table that will benefit your team and improve their lives.

It's important that you understand the above so you can have confidence when talking to a potential buyer/investor. Most owners are not aware of how to value their practice so they can get the best results for themselves and their team. **Remember, they will be working for the new owner.** Your best bet always is **keep asking, "How turnkey is my business? Can I go away for a month and the business still runs well, has high customer satisfaction and profit at 15-20%? Can problems be solved without me? Does my team collaborate well? What grade would I give our culture? Are we in synergy with AI & our Business Operating System? Know the answers to these questions and if your answers are no for some get to work!** Most buyers come along when the owner is unprepared. Don't let that be you.

Do you know the value of your practice? Would you like to get to know specifically what your practice is worth? I can help you with that. I work as a practice owner advocate to help you with all the questions and challenges that come up in business. I can work with you and show you what the value of your practice is with my practice valuation tools. **You can contact me, Mike Johnson at (847)-372-3432 or email me at askmj12@gmail.com.** I would be happy to help you.

9

Charting a Path to Future Success

I hope this guide has ignited a desire in you to embrace powerful, positive changes within your practice. Your veterinary practice isn't just a business; it's a platform to bring stability and security to your family, staff, and community. Remember, the Big Three—Security, Connection and Purpose—are what everyone seeks in their work today.

Embrace the seven systems and processes discussed in this book; **the potential rewards are significant, turning even a modest practice into a multi-million-dollar success story.** *Lena's journey exemplifies the profound impact of a strong culture and a committed team, driving growth and fulfillment.* Her team's dreams are realized not just within the practice, but as leaders and experts in their communities.

As you are aware, AI is advancing rapidly, offering both challenges and opportunities. Next-generation employees seek growth, mentorship, and coaching. Using potent operating systems like EOS, Pinnacle, Bloom Growth or a customized system built for your practice, they can greatly enhance your practice's efficiency and impact. *As a business coach, I've seen firsthand how these systems transform businesses, but the journey is difficult to navigate alone. This is where a coach's expertise becomes invaluable.*

We've also covered **how to evaluate and increase your practice's worth, particularly in the eyes of potential private equity buyers**. Understanding your practice's value is crucial, not just for selling, but for ensuring it aligns with good business operating systems and secure partnerships.

My passion lies in working with a select few clients who are driven to build exceptional veterinary practices for a greater purpose. The time to act is now. AI and modern practice management tools await implementation, setting the stage for your accelerated success.

For those **ready to take the next step**, I am here to offer support, guidance, and coaching to help you navigate this exciting journey. **Contact me at askmj12@gmail.com or call 847-372-3432.** You can also see me on LinkedIn (Michael R Johnson, MATL). Let's move forward together, transforming your business for long-lasting impact and success.

10

Conclusion Story & Contact information

As we draw this journey to a close, **I'd like to share a story with you from an inspiring chapter in my own life**. In my early years, I had the privilege of playing football at **Illinois Valley Community College**, under the guidance of **coach Vince McMahon**, a man who **embodied leadership, passion, and purpose**. His philosophy was simple yet profound: **practice as you play, cherish every victory, and develop the character needed to pursue significant goals.**

Our team, bound by hard work and camaraderie, achieved something pretty special. We went undefeated, winning the Midwest Bowl and earning honors that echo decades later. But beyond trophies and accolades, **what Vince instilled in us went far deeper. He taught us the value of teamwork, respect, and excellence—a legacy that extends far beyond the playing field.**

In the business world, much like sports, success is forged through the power of a cohesive, purpose-driven team. Every business is a tapestry of diverse talents, courage and unique strengths. As leaders, our role is to cultivate an environment where each team member can thrive and contribute to a shared vision. **Through effective coaching, we empower individuals with the skills, mindset, and resilience needed to succeed not just professionally but in life.**

Just as Vince knew that every win was a steppingstone to building a family of future leaders and coaches, we too **must recognize that our businesses are fertile grounds for growing talents and fostering lifelong friendships. When a team operates in harmony, embracing complementary strengths, they create a culture of collaboration, courage, creativity, and continual growth.**

And, like my experience on that unforgettable team, **your business can offer employees a platform where work becomes more than a job—it becomes a calling filled with joy, challenge, and achievement.** By nurturing such a team dynamic, **you're not only sculpting future successes but also crafting a legacy of empowered individuals who will carry forward these teachings into broader aspects of life. Pause and think about that for a minute.**

Through inspired leadership, we can provide the same gifts Vince bestowed upon us: **cherished memories, enduring relationships, and the skills to help others win.** A business led with purpose can change lives, one team member at a time. This is the ultimate testament to a fulfilling life—building great businesses for an even greater purpose.

Thank you for embarking on this journey to elevate your practice. May the strategies and stories shared within these pages inspire you to lead with vision, forge successful teams, and make an indelible difference in the world.

Again, For those **ready to take the next step**, I am here to offer support, guidance, and coaching to help you navigate this exciting journey. **Contact me at askmj12@gmail.com or call 847-372-3432.** You can also see me on Linked In (Michael R Johnson, MATL). Let's

CONCLUSION STORY & CONTACT INFORMATION

move forward together, transforming your business for long-lasting impact and success.

Leaders also understand the value of life long learning. By my association with the Global Leadership Summit, my Master's degree and my work with fellow coaches, I had the opportunity to ***learn from these great teachers. Here is the list of their books that help shape my work.*** I hope you will add them to your library and refer to them as often as I do.

- *Great By Choice* by Jim Collins
- *The Seven Habits of Highly Effective People* by Stephen R. Covey
- *The Speed of Trust* by Stephen M.R. Covey
- *The Advantage* by Patrick Lencioni
- *The Five Dysfunctions of a Team* by Patrick Lencioni
- *Crucial Conversations* by Joseph Grenny, Kerry Patterson, Ron McMillan, Al Switzler, and Emily Gregory
- *Death by Meeting* by Patrick Lencioni
- *Scaling Up* by Verne Harnish
- *Traction* by Gino Wickman
- *What the Heck is EOS* by Gino Wickman and Tom Bouwer
- *Strengths Based Leadership* by Tom Rath and Barry Conchie
- *Earn It* by Jill E. Young
- *Start With Why* by Simon Sinek
- *Lessons For Living: What Only Adversity Can Teach You* by Phil Stutz
- *The Tools: 5 Tools to Help You Find Courage, Creativity, and Willpower—and Inspire You to Live Your Life in Forward Motion* by Phil Stutz and Barry Michels

Phil & Barry's title really caps off my little book. May you find the courage, creativity and willpower to fully Live!

www.ingramcontent.com/pod-product-compliance
Lightning Source LLC
Chambersburg PA
CBHW071434220526
45469CB00004B/1528